A scene from the Yale Repertory Theatre Production of "Cobb." Set design by Rob Greenberg.

Photo by Rob Greenberg

COBB

BY LEE BLESSING

DRAMATISTS
PLAY SERVICE
INC.

Copyright © 1991, by Lee Blessing

All Rights Reserved

CAUTION: Professionals and amateurs are hereby warned that performance of COBB is subject to a royalty. It is fully protected under the copyright laws of the United States of America, and of all countries covered by the International Copyright Union (including the Dominion of Canada and the rest of the British Commonwealth), and of all countries covered by the Pan-American Copyright Convention, the Universal Copyright Convention, the Berne Convention, and of all countries with which the United States has reciprocal copyright relations. All rights, including professional/amateur stage rights, motion picture, recitation, lecturing, public reading, radio broadcasting, television, video or sound recording, all other forms of mechanical or electronic reproduction, such as CD-ROM, CD-I, information storage and retrieval systems and photocopying, and the rights of translation into foreign languages, are strictly reserved. Particular emphasis is laid upon the matter of readings, permission for which must be secured from the Author's agent in writing.

The stage performance rights in COBB (other than first class rights) are controlled exclusively by the DRAMATISTS PLAY SERVICE, INC., 440 Park Avenue South, New York, N.Y. 10016. No professional or non-professional performance of the Play (excluding first class professional performance) may be given without obtaining in advance the written permission of the DRAMATISTS PLAY SERVICE, INC., and paying the requisite fee.

Inquiries concerning all other rights should be addressed to Berman, Boals & Flynn, 225 Lafayette Street, suite 1207, New York, N.Y. 10012.

SPECIAL NOTE

Anyone receiving permission to produce COBB is required (1) to give credit to the Author as sole and exclusive Author of the Play on the title page of all programs distributed in connection with performances of the Play and in all instances in which the title of the Play appears for purposes of advertising, publicizing or otherwise exploiting the Play and/or a production thereof. The name of the Author must appear on a separate line, in which no other name appears, immediately beneath the title and in size of type equal to 50% of the largest, most prominent letter used for the title of the Play. No person, firm or entity may receive credit larger or more prominent than that accorded the Author, and (2) to give the following acknowledgments in all programs distributed in connection with performances of the Play:

Originally produced by Yale Repertory Theatre,
Lloyd Richards, Artistic Director.

Subsequently presented by
the Alliance Theatre Company, Atlanta, Georgia and
the Old Globe Theatre, San Diego, California.

*This play is dedicated to Jeanne Blake
and to Lloyd Richards*

COBB was produced at the Yale Repertory Theatre (Lloyd Richards, Artistic Director; Benjamin Mordecai, Managing Director), New Haven, Connecticut, on March 21, 1989. It was directed by Lloyd Richards; the set design was by Rob Greenberg; the costume design was by Joel O. Thayer; the lighting design was by Ashley York Kennedy; the sound design was by G. Thomas Clark; and the production stage manager was Maureen F. Gibson. The cast was as follows:

MR. COBB ....Josef Sommer
THE PEACH ....James E. Reynolds
TY ....Chris Cooper
OSCAR CHARLESTON ....Delroy Lindo

The Yale Repertory Theatre production of COBB was produced at the Alliance Theatre Company (Robert J. Farley, Artistic Director; Edith H. Love, Managing Director), Atlanta, Georgia, on May 6, 1990. It was directed by Lloyd Richards; the set design was by Rob Greenberg; the costume design was by Joel O. Thayer; the lighting design was by Ashley York Kennedy; the sound design was by G. Thomas Clark; original music was by Scott Davenport Richards; and the stage manager was Jonathan Dimock Secor. The cast was as follows:

MR. COBB ....William Newman
THE PEACH ....James E. Reynolds
TY ....George Gerdes
OSCAR CHARLESTON ....Dan Martin

The Yale Repertory Theatre production of COBB was produced at the Old Globe Theatre (Jack O'Brien, Artistic Director; Thomas Hall, Managing Director), San Diego, California, on June 28, 1990. It was directed by Lloyd Richards; the set design was by Rob Greenberg; the costume design was by Joel O. Thayer; the lighting design was by Ashley York Kennedy; the sound design was by G. Thomas Clark; original music was by Scott Davenport Richards; and the stage manager was Jonathan Dimock Secor. The cast was as follows:

MR. COBB .... William Newman
THE PEACH .... James E. Reynolds
TY .... George Gerdes
OSCAR CHARLESTON .... Dan Martin

CHARACTERS

THE PEACH — intense, athletic, quick to anger – about 20
TY — self-important, quick to anger – about 40
MR. COBB — bitter, quick to anger – over 70
OSCAR CHARLESTON — powerfully built, in his early 30's

TIME

1886-1961 and later

PLACE

Georgia, and elsewhere

COBB

(A narrow spot reveals Mr. Cobb, in a robe. He is autographing a baseball.)

MR. COBB. You think you invented me, but I invented you. You think this life you live is somehow your creation. It isn't. Everything about you started with men like me. The way you think, the world you live in — all of it shaped by men like me. We did our work in boardrooms, on Wall Street, in the White House — hell, even on the sports field. You think it's your national pastime. It isn't. It's mine. At the turn of the century I took a rustic, folk-art form called baseball and applied the science of warfare to it. Fit like a damn glove, you better believe. That's my contribution to America. That's what you owe me. I know these things for three reasons: I'm dead, I'm a millionaire, and I'm in the Hall of Fame. *(He suddenly stares out with surprise, and cocks his head as though listening. With a growing tone of accusation.)* You're trying to forget me. Aren't you? You're trying to forget me. You're trying to forget. *(Lights rise and follow Mr. Cobb to Peach, who sits on a bench, pulling up his socks. Peach wears the pants of a bright red baseball uniform. The shirt is on the bench. A bat leans against it. Peach speaks to the audience.)*

PEACH. *(With a noticeable Southern drawl.)* When I was sixteen I helped a doctor take a bullet out of a nigger some white boy had shot. I was tryin' to decide if I wanted to go into medicine. Dr. Moss had me give the boy chloroform and then feel around inside him. To find the bullet. 'Couldn't, though. Neither could Dr. Moss. We sewed him up again, and he lived ok, I guess. *(Holds up his hand, looks at it.)* My hands ... were covered in his blood. I'd felt all through him. *(Grimaces as he remembers.)* Lord, I thought I was going to throw up and faint all at the same time. *(Wiping his hands on his pants.)* I never became a doctor. Guess you can see that. Even so, blood has had a way of followin' me around. *(He stands, picks up the shirt.)* This here's the uniform of the Royston Reds. Of Royston, Georgia. When I was 14 I played my first game for 'em. Handled eight chances without an error, made three hits. Anyone who ever saw me play — ever — knew I was destined. *(Picks up the bat.)* Hell, I even made my own bat. In the town coffin-maker's shed. Used prime ash. *(Holds it out, testing its weight.)* Look at that. Baseball bat's a serious item. Now and again I think how many times one of these been used to kill somebody. It's a club, is what it is. People use it that way. In homes all over the nation. They club each other to death with the first thing comes to hand. *(He suddenly slams the bat hard against the bench, speaks quietly.)* I'm the greatest player that ever lived. Ty Cobb. My name's been on a lot of bats. So it's been covered in blood, I suppose — its share of the time. *(He makes to slam the bat against the bench again, but suddenly stops, relaxes.)* It's no toy. And it's no game, neither. *(He turns to go, stops.)* When I was 18, my mother killed my father. *(He hands the bat to Mr. Cobb and exits.)*

MR. COBB. There's no need to talk about it. *(Ty enters. He is dressed in a business suit, circa 1930. Ty's Southern accent is fainter than Peach's.)*

TY. Babe Ruth was an orphan, and America adopted him. My mother killed my father, and no one wants to know me.

MR. COBB. I told you, don't talk about it. Talk about my swing instead. *(Mr. Cobb tosses Ty the bat.)*

TY. Maybe you'd like to study my unique hand work. It's the secret of my success — along with the fact that I'm the most talented man ever to play the game.

MR. COBB. *(To the audience.)* Most talented. *(Ty gives him a look, then goes on demonstrating.)*

TY. See, I hold the hands apart. Then as I swing I move one hand towards the other, depending if I'm hitting to right or left. If you never played the game you don't know what I'm talking about, and if you have, you can't do it as well as me anyway. So don't try to analyze it. Just remember it's part of my myth.

MR. COBB. Any great myth needs a great beginning. It's like the advice I give young boys I'm teaching how to hit: First of all, get yourself a comfortable stance. It's my first rule for young ballplayers. *(Ty assumes his typical stance. He lets the bat drop to his shoulder.)*
TY. My mother took a lover. That's what some people said.
MR. COBB. I said don't talk about — *(Ty silences him with a look. To audience.)*
TY. Personally I think it's a *goddamn vicious lie,* but they said it. *(Peach reemerges at the side of the stage.)*
PEACH. Whole town said it.
TY. Liar. *(To audience.)* My father was W.H. Cobb. People called him Professor. School commissioner, newspaper editor, state senator. When he was 21 he married my mother.
PEACH. She was 12.
TY. What the hell's wrong with that?! *(A beat.)* I was playing with the Augusta Tourists in the Sally League. It was 1905. One night, down in Royston, my father said he was going out to the farm for a couple days.
PEACH. He wasn't, though.
MR. COBB. *(To audience.)* This is hearsay. I heard all this later.
TY. He took the buggy and left my mother alone in the house. My brother and sister were away at friends'. Later, Mama locked the windows upstairs in the bedroom —
PEACH. Even though it was August, in Georgia —
MR. COBB. All hearsay. We'll never really know.
TY. She was afraid of being alone. She went to bed.
PEACH. 'Bout that time someone saw my father. He wasn't out at the farm like he said. He was in town. Just walkin' by himself. And he had a gun.
MR. COBB. All this was years ago.
TY. Little after midnight my mother heard a noise outside her window, out on the porch roof. Someone was trying to open the window. She was all alone in the house.
PEACH. She said she was alone. There was a gun in the room.
TY. A shotgun.
MR. COBB. That's not unusual.
PEACH. Papa kept it there, for times of danger.

TY. She picked it up. She couldn't tell who was at the window.
PEACH. Did she look?
TY. She was afraid to look.
PEACH. Maybe she already knew.
TY. That's a heartless lie! How can you even think that?!
PEACH. I can't help what I think! There ain't no way of really knowin'!
MR. COBB. *(To audience.)* It's all conjecture.
TY. Then think the best!
MR. COBB. That's a good idea. Why don't we just —
PEACH. Why'd she need to do anything? Tell me that. The window was locked.
TY. Whoever it was could've smashed the window.
PEACH. So she just fired? She didn't look? It could've been anybody.
TY. *That's right! It could've been anybody!*
MR. COBB. *(To audience.)* It was so long ago.
TY. She was alone. She fired.
PEACH. She said she was alone.
TY. Later, she fired again. But not for a little while, people said. Not for a little while.
PEACH. Outside the window, on the porch roof — with all that broken glass — that's where my father died.
TY. He was shot in the stomach — and in the head.
PEACH. The neighbors ran over. They found a gun in my father's pocket.
MR. COBB. Well fine. Now you've told it. Let's move on.
TY. My mother was arrested. Accused of voluntary manslaughter.
PEACH. After the funeral, I stayed with her. Four days. Listenin' to her ... tell her story. It never got any clearer. I mean it made sense, sort of. She was alone. I've been alone like that. At the same time, what if there was a lover?
TY. *There was no lover!*
PEACH. *(To the audience.)* Would you believe her?
TY. I did!
PEACH. And I didn't. Whatever the truth was, my mother

killed my father. And everything I ever thought or did or said after that, knew that. *(Ty regards Peach for a moment, then stalks out. Lights fade out on Peach.)*
MR. COBB. The son of a homicide. See, that's what I mean about a myth. It's got to have the right kind of start. Look at Babe Ruth. He had a beautiful myth: in a home for wayward boys from the age of seven. His folks couldn't handle him. A priest became his second father. Boy hero rises from nothing. Horatio Alger couldn't have written it better. What did I have? A goddamn Greek tragedy. Where the hell was my second father? *(Lights expand to reveal a brown paper sack with a Luger pistol on top of it.)* What do you think's in the bag? You can see what's on top of the bag. What do you think's in it? *(A beat.)* What would you have in it? *(He picks up the gun, taps the bag with it.)* One million dollars in negotiable securities. The gun's real, by the way. Don't get any ideas. *(Sitting.)* I had a little touch of cancer. Prostate cancer, at first. Cancer of everything else, eventually. It climbed its way up my back, into my brain. Took nearly two years. I fought it on my own, but finally the pain got too bad, and I ... came here. They shot me full of drugs. I was unconscious for a few weeks, and then I died. And dreamed. *(Oscar Charleston enters, approaches Mr. Cobb from behind. Charlestown wears the white baseball uniform of the 1921 Indianapolis ABCs. Mr. Cobb senses him without turning.)* Who are you?
CHARLESTON. Nobody special. *(He rubs Mr. Cobb's shoulders.)*
MR. COBB. You an orderly?
CHARLESTON. Not exactly. Name's Charleston.
MR. COBB. Charleston?
CHARLESTON. That's right. Oscar Charleston.
MR. COBB. *(With a trace of recognition.)* Charleston — ?
CHARLESTON. You got yourself a nice setup here, Mr. Cobb. Soft bed, nice quiet room, plenty of money. Looks like you died real good here.
MR. COBB. *(Still trying to place the name.)* Oscar Charleston.... Do I know you?
CHARLESTON. Hard to say who knows me. It's very important to die good. It's your last thing — your very last memory

before ... Well, before you know it. Man, you got some tight muscles.
MR. COBB. *(Shrugging his hands away.)* Damn it, tell me who you are!
CHARLESTON. Look for yourself. *(Mr. Cobb stands, looks around at Charleston for the first time.)*
MR. COBB. A ballplayer? You played ball?
CHARLESTON. More'n 20 years.
MR. COBB. You're not old enough.
CHARLESTON. Thought you'd like to see me in my prime. I can be older if you want.
MR. COBB. Charleston ... What position did you play?
CHARLESTON. Center field, same as you. Sit back down now. Or you in so much comfort around here you don't need a back rub? *(Slowly, Mr. Cobb sits. Charleston resumes rubbing his shoulders.)*
MR. COBB. A ballplayer. Were you any good?
CHARLESTON. *(Laughing softly.)* Better'n you.
MR. COBB. *No one was better than me!* *(Charleston squeezes the top of Mr. Cobb's shoulder hard.)* OW!!
CHARLESTON. Sorry. To tell the truth, I was about the finest ever played. I could hit to all fields, hit with power — run a fly ball down like it was a hundred dollar bill. Folks said it was a privilege to watch me play.
MR. COBB. If you're so good, why don't I remember you?
CHARLESTON. You never would've played against me. Not back then.
MR. COBB. *(Trying to remember.)* Oscar Charleston...
CHARLESTON. It'll come back. Everything comes back — that's the truest thing I know. *(He finishes rubbing, starts to leave.)* How's that now?
MR. COBB. What?
CHARLESTON. Feel better?
MR. COBB. *(Absently.)* Oh. Yes, it does.
CHARLESTON. Thank you.
MR. COBB. What?
CHARLESTON. I rubbed your back. Say thank you.
MR. COBB. Oh ... Thank you.

CHARLESTON. You're welcome. I'll be back later. *(Charleston starts out.)*
MR. COBB. Wait a minute — where are you going?
CHARLESTON. Don't worry. I'll be around.
MR. COBB. Charleston — wait! Charleston!
CHARLESTON. *(As he goes.)* One thing you can count on — I'll always be around.
MR. COBB. Why don't I remember you!? *(Ty enters as Charleston exits. Charleston gives Ty an easy wave as they pass. Ty still has the bat.)*
TY. Who was that?
MR. COBB. I don't know. I don't ... recall. *(Mr. Cobb continues to stare off after Charleston. Ty stares at him.)*
TY. I was going to talk now.
MR. COBB. What?
TY. I was going to talk now. All right?
MR. COBB. *(Still distracted.)* What about?
TY. My money.
MR. COBB. What? Yes — Fine, good. Stick to the subject. *(Mr. Cobb stares off as before. Ty speaks to the audience.)*
TY. When I died my estate was worth anywhere from six to ten million dollars, depending on which self-interested sonofabitch you asked. I kept score with two things in life: with this ... *(Indicates the bat.)* And with money. Did just as well with both. Tell me — what would you do if you were a young ballplayer in Detroit in the first twenty years of this century? You'd invest in General Motors, of course. My Lord, it was like opening your door and having money pour in your house. Yet how many of my Tiger teammates made that same investment? The stupid sonsabitches could've been rich! *I* told 'em how! Ballplayers are the most ignorant class of creatures on the face of creation.
MR. COBB. Except for sportswriters.
TY. I told them, too. Might as well have asked 'em to invest in Bolshevism. In 1918 I invested in Coca-Cola. You think those sportswriters would go into it?
MR. COBB. Coca-Cola in 1918. You bet I was rich. I retired as the first millionaire ballplayer, decades before anyone else

did it.
TY. Investing wasn't hard. Hitting a spitter was hard. To make money, get hold of one simple thing — and never let it go.
MR. COBB. Self-made millionaire. In an age of millionaires — that's what I was. That's my myth. I helped shape the American Age. No one's going to forget that. *(To audience.) You're not going to forget that. (Mr. Cobb snaps his fingers. A projection appears U. It is Ty Cobb, full-figure, in a Detroit Tigers uniform, circa 1905. Mr. Cobb smiles, then looks expectantly toward the wings. A moment passes.)* Well? Where the hell are you? *(Peach enters, wearing the same Tigers uniform. On his shoulders are three bats. He stares at Mr. Cobb.)*
PEACH. What'll I talk about?
MR. COBB. About the uniform, damn it — what do you think? *(Peach addresses the audience.)*
PEACH. Like this uniform? The Detroit Tigers were the last team to keep full collars on their shirts. Comes from a time when players wore ties, pitched underhand and hit with flat bats. The game was half gentleman, half farmboy — it never really knew what it wanted to be. Till I came along.
TY. I was the quickest, meanest, smartest, fiercest, *best* man ever to play the game. I took baseball exactly like a man takes a wife. I made it mine.
MR. COBB. Before me, baseball was a virgin. When I was through, it was American. *(Ty exits. Mr. Cobb stays to watch Peach.)*
PEACH. I was the first man ever to swing three bats in the on-deck circle. Made the one bat feel lighter when I hit. The other Tigers thought I was tryin' to show 'em up. I wasn't. I was just gettin' ready to take their job. These bats are the ones I made down in Royston. Later on in my first year here someone cut 'em all in half. For a joke. *(He sets two of the bats aside.)* I had 'em for my first game, though. August 30th, 1905. We were playing the New York Highlanders, which is what they called the Yankees then. Happy Jack Chesbro was the pitcher. Spitballer. The year before, he won 41 games — which is a hell of a lot of spit. *(Standing at an invisible home plate.)* Bottom of the first inning I got up with a man on third and two outs. I

stared out at that Hall of Fame pitcher, and he stared back at me like I wasn't there. He threw the first pitch high and I missed it, and he started to smile. Then he threw a curveball that broke right over the outside corner and froze my blood for strike two, and he moved up to a happy little grin. Old Jack was gettin' ready to laugh me right out of there, but I was calm as the Dead Sea. I knew this game was invented for me, and not for Happy Jack Chesbro. On the next pitch, I swung again — and lined one hard to left-center, and took second on what rightly would've been a single for any other man and got the first run batted in of my career all in the very same moment of time. *(A beat.)* And when Jack Chesbro looked around at me, standing on second base, he was lookin' at his future. Not so long after that they started callin' me the Georgia Peach.

MR. COBB.   A great myth needs a great name. I had a great name. The Georgia Peach.

PEACH.   That was three weeks after my mother killed my father. *(Peach turns and exits, carrying the bats.)*

MR. COBB.   You know, you can't overstress the positive in baseball. A positive frame of mind — that's everything. That's why a great name is important. The Georgia Peach. It meant perfection. I became perfection. *(Lights rise on Ty. He is now in 1930's North American hunting garb. He is cleaning a big-game rifle.)*

TY.   In the spring they put my mother on trial.

MR. COBB.   Leave it alone.

TY.   Why?

MR. COBB.   There's no way to win with something like that.

TY.   'Course there is. It was a trial. Somebody wins, somebody loses. *(To audience.)* It wasn't long, only lasted a couple days. I tried to get there on time, but I couldn't.

PEACH.   *(Reentering.)* I didn't want to.

TY.   That's a lie.

MR. COBB.   There's no need to —

PEACH.   I stayed at spring trainin' long as I could. Who in hell wants to hear their mother testify about a thing like that?

TY.   *I* did!

PEACH.   Then why wasn't I there?

TY. I heard the final summations the next day.
MR. COBB. That's enough!
TY. Lasted more than five hours. Then the jury retired. *One hour* later they came back in. Not guilty.
PEACH. Not guilty.
MR. COBB. Not guilty.
PEACH. Nobody, in that whole trial, ever once mentioned a lover.
TY. There was no lover! She told me!
PEACH. Over and over she told me. In her way. And did I believe her?
TY. Yes!
PEACH. No!
MR. COBB. *(To audience.)* A positive frame of mind. The most important thing in baseball. Now let's change the subject.
TY. To what?
MR. COBB. I don't know — guns. You're standing there with a big-game rifle, for God's sake.
TY. *(To audience.)* I grew up with guns. Liked to hunt, all my life. Shot game in the Tetons, California —
MR. COBB. *(To audience.)* Hunting was very popular then —
TY. You want me to talk or not? *(To audience.)* I shot bear, moose, caribou. Nothing compared with hunting. Once, in Canada, I got lost. Wandered around in that wilderness for two days 'til I found the railroad. Totally cut off from the world of men. *(Pauses, recalling it.)* Best two days I ever spent. *(He slams the rifle's bolt shut.)*
MR. COBB. Don't say that. That's not true.
TY. What do you mean it's not true?
MR. COBB. It's not. I liked being around people. Liked it a lot. *(To Peach.)* Didn't I?
TY. I did, eh? That why I roomed alone so much on the road?
MR. COBB. That wasn't other people, that was ballplayers. Because of the hazing my rookie year, that's all. *(To Peach.)* Tell 'em!
TY. *Hazing?* That what you call it? They made me feel like an animal. *(To Peach.)* Didn't they!?
MR. COBB. It was the way then. You're there to replace one

of 'em — they don't take kindly to it. Doesn't mean you hate all humanity.
TY. It doesn't?
MR. COBB. *(To Peach.)* Hazing wasn't so bad. It was just the first season, first ... couple, maybe. They didn't do anything so bad — what'd they do? Lock me out of the hotel bathroom. Not speak to me —
PEACH. Nail my shoes to the floor.
TY. Saw my bats in half, attack me on the train —
MR. COBB. It wasn't that bad. It was a team, it was —
TY. I felt like an animal! Hell, I learned what "team" meant — it meant them against me. I was humiliated every day by players not fit to stand on the same field with me.
MR. COBB. *(To Peach.)* Everybody else took it —
PEACH. I wasn't everybody else!
TY. They could see that. Only made 'em more vicious.
MR. COBB. You're concentrating on the wrong things —
TY. Tell 'em what I did.
MR. COBB. We don't have to —
TY. Tell 'em! I did the only thing a sane man would do. I bought a gun. Made a new rule for young ballplayers.
PEACH. Always keep a lethal weapon within reach.
MR. COBB. No —
TY. We're telling the truth here. If we're talking about my life, it's going to be the truth.
MR. COBB. Not all the truth. We can't —
TY. All of it: arguments, suspensions, fights —
MR. COBB. What good'll that do?! That's not what people want to hear about.
TY. It's all they want to hear about. *(To audience.)* I fought people. I don't mean shoving matches, I mean fights: blood, bruises, broken bones — people laid up for days. Careers ended. I had fights.
MR. COBB. On the field, he means. It was a kind of strategy —
TY. Not strategy. Not just on the field — *fights!*
MR. COBB. Every man has fights. We wouldn't be human if —

TY. October 6, 1906.
MR. COBB. Don't go into this.
TY. October 6, 1906. Come on. It's who I was.
MR. COBB. *(To Peach.)* It doesn't have to be!
PEACH. October 6, 1906. A low-skunk pitcher named Ed Siever — my own teammate — hit me from behind in a hotel lobby.
TY. I decked him with one punch, then hit him a few more in the jaw, then I kicked him a few in the head for good measure.
MR. COBB. I never kicked him.
TY. I only kicked him a few.
MR. COBB. *I never kicked him.*
TY. How the hell do you know?! You don't remember what happened!
MR. COBB. What I remember *is* what happened! *(A beat. To Ty.)* Don't you see how it works?
TY. *(To audience.)* That night on the train, I lay awake in my berth with a pistol in my hand.
PEACH. *(Producing a pistol.)* Baseball was a team game. That was its only flaw.
TY. March, 1907.
MR. COBB. Stop this.
TY. I got blindsided by a homicidal catcher named Charley Schmidt.
PEACH. He didn't blindside me.
TY. Hell, he didn't. How else could that dumbass get me on the ground?
MR. COBB. *(To them both.)* Charley Schmidt was nobody.
PEACH. *(To Ty.)* He was bigger than me.
TY. What's that got to do with it!?
PEACH. *(To the audience.)* Charley Schmidt once fought Jack Johnson. For fun, he used to pound nails in the clubhouse floor with his fist.
TY. He never hurt me.
PEACH. He broke my nose.
TY. He never — !!
MR. COBB. *(Simultaneously with Ty's line.)* Stop this! *(Ty bran-*

dishes his rifle threateningly at Peach just as Mr. Cobb reaches for his Luger attempting to get them both to stop. Peach instantly points his pistol at them both. They all freeze for a moment, nervous and embarrassed.)
MR. COBB. Look at us. It's like a damn armory out here. *(Mr. Cobb takes Ty's rifle and shoves it into Peach's grasp.)* Get rid of these. *(Peach exits with the pistol and rifle. Mr. Cobb speaks to the audience, gesticulating with the Luger, which is still in his hand.)* I never owned a gun in my life! *(Becoming conscious of the Luger once more, putting it in his robe pocket.)* That was a ... mistake, that fight with Charley Schmidt. Happened off the field. It had nothing to do with science, or strategy or anything useful. I've decided to disown it.
TY. Disown it?
MR. COBB. That's right. It's ... not worth recalling from the past, so it's no longer part of the past. Simple as that.
TY. And that makes it disappear? It never happened?
MR. COBB. It never happened. It was a lie someone told.
TY. *(As Peach reenters, sans guns.)* You intend to just re-remember everything?
MR. COBB. Not everything. I admit to plenty of fights — in games. Fair fights, where I had a plan and a goal. Like how about that time I crashed into that catcher and he dropped the ball and I scored?
PEACH. The one who got so mad he started hittin' me on the head with the ball? Oh, that's a hell of a fight: me lyin' on the plate, him smackin' me on the head.
MR. COBB. But I scored! That's the point. My strategy was successful. I got the best of it — somehow.
TY. Why's that matter so much?
MR. COBB. What do you mean?
TY. Why's it matter who won? It was a fight — I fought. That's who I was.
MR. COBB. No, I won — *that's* who I was. *(Charleston appears, still in the Indianapolis ABC's uniform. He carries a mop and silently mops the floor as he goes — no bucket, a dry mop.)* What are you doing here?
CHARLESTON. Heard you talkin' about fights.

MR. COBB. So what?
CHARLESTON. Didn't want you to forget old Bungy, that's all.
MR. COBB. Bungy?
CHARLESTON. You remember Bungy. Colored fella. Groundskeeper at your spring training field, down in Augusta.
MR. COBB. I never fought with Bungy.
CHARLESTON. *(To Ty, not unpleasantly, as he mops.)* Sure you did. You chased him all over the field that day he come up to you drunk, kept calling you Carrie 'stead of your right name.
TY. I don't remember that.
CHARLESTON. "Carrie!" he said. "Carrie," 'stead of Cobb. 'Stead of *Mr.* Cobb. You can't forget that.
MR. COBB. I forget what I like.
CHARLESTON. You chased him all over, finally caught him by the clubhouse. His wife came out, started yelling at you to let him go.
MR. COBB. *(To Peach.)* Get him outta here.
CHARLESTON. Then you started choking her. Bungy's wife. You started choking her.
TY. This is lies.
CHARLESTON. *(Maintaining his pleasant tone.)* No, it ain't. They had to pull you away.
MR. COBB. I don't even know who you are.
CHARLESTON. Choking a woman like that. You amazed everybody that day.
PEACH. I didn't choke her hard.
MR. COBB. Don't admit it!
PEACH. I was just holdin' her neck, that's all — to keep her off me.
CHARLESTON. *(To Peach.)* I believe you. You ain't got to convince me.
MR. COBB. Why'd you bring this up?
CHARLESTON. I was afraid you'd forget it — it being preseason and all.
TY. *(Pulling the mop away from Charleston.)* Who the hell are you, anyway? *(Charleston is silent.)* Who!!?
MR. COBB. Oscar Charleston, whoever that is.

CHARLESTON. You probably think of me by a different name. That's why you don't remember. You need that key name. You think of that, and you'll know who I am.
TY. I will?
CHARLESTON. *(Taking the mop back gently.)* You should. World of baseball ain't that big, after all. Still, it's hard to remember sometimes. Man gets old, his memory starts to get smaller. *(As he mops.)* Oh, his mind keeps working at it — goes over and over things. Kind of like a guard in an army camp, checking the perimeter wire. Round and round he goes, checking. But maybe someone's moving that wire in on him. Maybe he doesn't even notice. He just keeps going around, and all the time that wire's moving in a little bit more, and a little bit more, and a little bit —
MR. COBB. I am not absent-minded!
CHARLESTON. Never said you were.
MR. COBB. *(Confronting Charleston.)* If I don't know you, it's because I didn't need to know you. Didn't care to. You weren't important.
CHARLESTON. *(Smiling.)* Maybe you're right. Got to admit I always thought I was important: Oscar McKinley Charleston, born October, 1896. McKinley was running for President. That's how I got a mountain for my middle name. I did think I was someone. Suppose we all do.
TY. I *was* someone.
CHARLESTON. I know. Nothing changes that, even if you do want to block me out of your mind.
TY. I'm not blocking anybody out of anything! Now you get the hell out of here, or I'll —
PEACH. I remember him. *(All look at Peach. Charleston smiles.)* I know who he is. Just didn't want to say it. Oscar McKinley Charleston. He's the Black Cobb.
MR. COBB. *(With a look at Charleston.)* The Black Cobb?
TY. *(With disgusted recognition.)* The Black Cobb.
CHARLESTON. *(Quietly sliding the mop into Ty's hand.)* It's a pleasure to be recognized. *(Charleston exits.)*
PEACH. What the hell is he doin' here, anyway?
MR. COBB. How should I know?

TY. *(Throwing down the mop, starting out.)* The Black Cobb. I'll beat his damn head in.
MR. COBB. No! Leave him alone.
TY. *(Stopping.)* Why?
MR. COBB. 'Cause I say so. *(Ty returns to the others.)*
TY. All that stuff about Bungy. As though he never had any fights — what the hell's he doing here!?
PEACH. Moppin' up. *(Ty suddenly throws the mop far into the darkness.)*
TY. *Keep away from me! You hear!!?*
MR. COBB. There's no reason we have to pay attention to him. He's got nothing to say that's relevant anyhow. We'll just ignore him.
TY. Ignore him?!
MR. COBB. That's right. A man that needs a name like that just to be remembered. *(Charleston reenters and stands a short distance from the others. They stare at him. He stares back. Mr. Cobb pulls the others away from him.)* I said ignore him. *(A moment passes. Irresistibly, the three of them slowly turn their heads and look at Charleston again. He smiles.)*
TY. *(To Peach.)* You had to go and remember him —
MR. COBB. Don't think about him and he'll go; it's as simple as that. Talk about something else. Anything — it doesn't matter.
TY. Fights?
MR. COBB. No —
PEACH. Yeah, fights.
MR. COBB. I — all right, if it'll keep our minds off ... Go ahead: name a fight, any fight.
TY. Any fight?
MR. COBB. Not *any* fight.
CHARLESTON. May 15, 1912. *(They turn and look at Charleston.)*
MR. COBB. Why that one?
CHARLESTON. Why not?
MR. COBB. *(To the others again.)* Something else. A different fight.
PEACH. Why not that one?
MR. COBB. 'Cause I say so.

TY. It's as good as any other. Hell, better.
MR. COBB. I always get the worst of that one. Come off sounding like a monster.
TY. Damn it, *I'm me! (To audience.)* May 15, 1912. Put yourself in my place. For seven years you're the finest player in baseball. Better hitter, better runner, better fielder, better *thinker* than any man who's played the game. If an outfielder was slow throwing a ball in, I took an extra base. If someone got in my way, I knocked 'em down. If they blocked a base, I spiked 'em. If they wanted to fight over it, I fought 'em. *Any*one. That was the bargain I'd made with baseball. If I was destined to play a child's game all my life, at least I was going to play it like an adult.
PEACH. *(To audience.)* What he means is, I beat up a fan.
TY. There's no damn dignity in the game! None! When I started in the big leagues, they put fans right in the outfield with you. Just roped 'em off behind you, like patrons at a movie theater. Someone'd hit a long fly ball, you'd have to go tearing through a bunch of strangers to get it. Dangerous as hell. Owners didn't care.
PEACH. It was worse when you played away.
TY. Think about it. 5,000 strangers standin' right behind you, so close they can touch you — all of 'em rootin' for the other team.
MR. COBB. They weren't the worst, though.
PEACH. No, they weren't.
TY. The worst are the ones who sit in the grandstand, right by your bench. They feel protected, behind a railing. Like little kings — them sitting, you standing up all day. The worst of the worst come back every game, sit in the same place, shout the same vileness, the same humiliations. I can think of no other art form — and baseball, as I played it, was an art form — in which ignoramuses are expected to scream insults in your face on a daily basis. Hell, Beethoven'd kill a man for that!
MR. COBB. *(Subdued.)* What are they thinking, when they shout those things? What's in their minds, what's in their hearts, that makes them need to pull a man down? It's anonymous — there's no real triumph in it. They shout from a

crowd.

PEACH. They're cowards, is all. We're all cowards, only some of us do it in public. *(Suddenly shouting, like a fan.)* Hey, *Cobb!* You ice wagon! Your *mother* can run better'n you!

MR. COBB. *(Shouting.)* Your *mother* can do everything better'n you!

TY. *(Shouting.)* And she can do it more often!

MR. COBB. *(Shouting.)* With more people!

PEACH. *(Shouting.)* AND SHE CAN MAKE MORE MONEY AT IT!!!

TY. *(Shouting.)* Your mother!

TY and PEACH. *(Louder.)* Your mother!!

TY, PEACH and MR. COBB. *(Shouting together.)* YOUR MOTHER!!

PEACH. They *can* go too far.

TY. But you bear it. As much as possible, anyway.

PEACH. Till you can't anymore.

MR. COBB. Till you can't anymore.

CHARLESTON. May 15,1912. *(Charleston moves to the background.)*

TY. Claude Lueker.

PEACH. Claude Lueker.

MR. COBB. I won't even say his name.

TY. A law clerk. Not even a clerk. A flunky.

MR. COBB. New York. It always happens in New York. That city was made for dishonorable encounters.

PEACH. Game after game he came. Whenever we played there. I was his only target. He was a specialist.

TY. They pick you out. They choose you alone. That more than anything is why you hate them. Claude Lueker.

PEACH. He was deformed — that's what I remember. Lost one of his hands in an accident. Plus part of the other. He was deformed on the inside and out.

TY. Many times I ignored him. Whole games. Whole series. I shouted back, but I never crossed that railing. How would it look, going after a crippled man? I held myself back.

PEACH. But then he figured out something new to say.

TY. He should never have said it.

MR. COBB. He should never have thought he could get away with saying it.
PEACH. He should've known. I'm a Georgian. He should've known.
TY. *(Almost unable to say it.)* He called me a ... a "half-nigger." *(Charleston laughs.)*
PEACH. And up I went — over that railing! Hell, I'da jumped over the Earth to get that man!
MR. COBB. Twelve rows!
TY. Twelve rows!
PEACH. I went like a shot! His throat was big and white as the moon.
TY. I was bigger than him, I was stronger than him, and dammit, I was better than him! I punched him, I threw him down —
MR. COBB. I kicked him — I never kicked that other fellow, but I kicked Claude Lueker!
TY. I kicked him!
PEACH. I kicked him hard. Nobody could pull me off him!
TY. And suddenly someone screamed, "Stop it! He has no hands!"
PEACH. And I never paused. I just kept kicking!
TY. I shouted back —
MR. COBB. *"I don't care if he has no feet!!!"* *(A beat. Charleston exits.)* I should never have remembered that one.
PEACH. Why? 'Cause it made me feel so right?
MR. COBB. I was not right.
PEACH. Hell, I wasn't. *(To audience.)* You think I was right, don't you? *(With a dismissive wave.)* Aw, the crowd'll always side with the cripple. But if I wasn't right, why did every one of the Tigers back what I'd done? Men who didn't even like me.
MR. COBB. *(To Peach.)* They were my teammates —
TY. *(To Mr. Cobb.)* They hated my guts. *(To audience.)* But when I got suspended for that fight, they walked off the field for me. Held the first-ever wildcat strike in baseball on my account.
PEACH. *(To audience.)* Manager had to hire local semipro and college players to wear our uniforms and play the Athletics in

our place. Athletics beat 'em 24 to 2. Guess that taught everybody.
TY. *(To audience.)* More important, every congressman from Georgia wired me congratulations. The mayor and police chief of Atlanta both supported me. The police chief said if I hadn't done what I'd done, I'd've "lost the respect of every decent man in the country."
PEACH. In 1912 in this country, you knew where people stood.
TY. March 31, 1917.
MR. COBB. Hold on!
TY. Why? We're just getting rolling. March 31, 19 —
MR. COBB. *Stop it! Now! (A beat.)* Don't you see what this is doing? And he just loves it, that Charleston, didn't you hear him? I will not permit an unbalanced view. It's that damn simple. I did not just fight people. I ... loved, and I gave away money ... near the end, and I had friends and family. I was a normal man. Who's going to remember me if they think I was a monster? They'll toss me away. They'll keep Ruth — that's what they'll do. Him they'll remember for centuries. Me... *(Trails off, quieter.)* He's the one. He's the goddamn mountain. *(Mr. Cobb sits tiredly as a projection of Babe Ruth's face fills the area behind them. Ty and Peach regard Mr. Cobb.)*
TY. *(To audience.)* It's not easy to be dethroned. I played big-league ball for ten years before Ruth showed up. By then I was king. I'd already won eight straight batting titles. Hell, in 1911 Shoeless Joe Jackson hit .408 and I *still* beat him for the title, with .420. I even led the league in homers once. Had 9 one year — and was proud of every one of 'em. Then in 1920, Ruth hit 54. *(We hear the crack of a bat, a crowd roars.)* 54 home runs. No one had ever come near that. Overnight, people went crazy for home runs. They went crazy for him, too. Didn't matter if I could do everything there was in the game. As far as the fans were concerned, he only had to do one thing.
MR. COBB. God, how they loved him. They stared into that stupid meatface of his and saw ... something. Not intelligence, I'll tell you that. I mean, if you had a company to run, who would you pick to run it — him or me? No contest.

PEACH. So what was it? Not good manners. Not sobriety, neither. Ruth wasn't guilty of any form of clean livin'.

TY. What made people think of that face — only that face, nothing more — whenever you mentioned baseball? What on earth did he have?

MR. COBB. Charm.

PEACH. And timin'. The sonofabitch hit his stride right after World War I — right when the baseball got livelier, more fans were comin' in, new parks were bein' built —

TY. Location. That's what it was. In 1920 the Red Sox sold him to the Yankees. It's one thing to be the best, but to be the best in New York. *(As the projection slowly begins to fade.)*

MR. COBB. But when you analyze it — when you really analyze it — what exactly did he offer? I mean, look at a typical trip to the plate for Babe Ruth. What happens? He takes a cut, hits a home run, trots his way around the basepath like a big cow without a thought in his head. That's no trip around the bases.

PEACH. *(To the audience.)* I'll show you a trip around the bases. Cobb-style. It starts with a few carefully-chosen words to the opposin' pitcher. Things like, "Hey, Rag-arm! That can't be your fastball. You sure you're not a left-hander?" If you make him feel bad enough about one of his pitches, you can bet that's what he'll throw you next time.

TY. *(Having picked up a bat, demonstrating.)* Then you decide which way you're going to hit it. If there's a man on, you want to pull, hit behind him — so you bring that left hand down and swing away.

PEACH. *(With a bat, demonstrating.)* If he's fast — and this guy's not, or you wouldn't goad him into giving you the fastball in the first place — you'd bring your right hand up and punch it the other way.

MR. COBB. Either way, you hit a liner — not some soft, lazy high fly that flops into the stands someplace. No. You hit a bullet. You sizzle it past the pitcher's ear — terrify the man. Make him forget all about winning. Make him glad just to be alive.

TY. Even though you've got a base hit, you run to first like you're legging out a triple.

PEACH. Just the sight of speed can demoralize the other team. If you're fast with your body, it stands to reason you're fast with your mind — or you'd slow down, and not get hurt.

TY. Once you're on first, you start to systematically destroy the pitcher's mind. It's not hard. If he had much of a mind, he wouldn't be a pitcher. Hell, Babe himself was a pitcher to begin with, and I hit .326 off him.

MR. COBB. You take a lead off first.

PEACH. A big lead. So he'll throw over.

TY. And he does! And you dive back, and you just make it.

MR. COBB. All the rubes in the stands think he got the best of that one, but he didn't.

PEACH. You saw his best move.

TY. You measured him. You can predict him now.

PEACH. And when he does that little thing — whatever it is — makes that tiny, unconscious gesture that means he's going home and not to first...

MR. COBB. *You take off!*

TY. You use the best speed in the league tearing for second base!

PEACH. And that catcher sees you go, and his heart turns to a cinder, 'cause he knows you already got the base stole on the pitcher's move.

TY. But he knows he's got to throw it anyway, so's not to look like a coward.

MR. COBB. *No mercy for cowards!*

PEACH. So he throws to second. And that ball is screamin' in from home, and I'm screamin' in from first — and sometimes I really am screamin' — and that second baseman knows everything there is to know about my spikes.

TY. I sharpen my spikes on the dugout steps for all to see.

MR. COBB. That's the legend.

TY. And I like it!

PEACH. He's gotta get that throw. But he's gotta watch my spikes!

MR. COBB. I'll cut him to pieces.

TY. I've done it before.

PEACH. The throw's low! He jumps away too soon!
TY. The ball goes into center field!
MR. COBB. And I head for third!
PEACH. But the center-fielder knows who I am! He's playin' shallow. He's got a play on me at third. All he needs to do is throw it on the money and I'll be out. I will be, too! He's got a good arm!
TY. So I look at the third baseman. I look at his eyes! He's gettin' ready. He sees me comin', he sees the ball, he watches the ball and *I watch his eyes!*
MR. COBB. And I line my body up with his eyes — so when that ball comes, it'll never get to him. It'll hit me in the back, instead. It'll hit *me!* And *I'll get my base!*
PEACH. *(Quietly, intently.)* The basepaths belong to me.
TY. They belong to me.
MR. COBB. They're mine.
PEACH. Safe at third. On a single. But not home yet.
TY. I look at the pitcher. His face is like the bottom of a metal bucket. He's not thinking anymore. He's not feeling, either. I'm just doing things to him.
MR. COBB. On the very next pitch, I take a long, walking lead off third. When the pitcher goes home, so do I.
PEACH. There's no pleasure on earth like stealin' home. My wedding night was nothing compared to stealing home.
TY. It's just you, the ball and the catcher.
PEACH. You can't beat the ball to home. If it's a decent pitch at all, you can't beat it to the plate. You got to force your way in.
MR. COBB. It's the catcher or you, that's what it is. It's a fight.
TY. If he drops the ball you're safe. If he doesn't —
PEACH. You got to force your way in. You got to need to win.
TY. You got to do *any*thing. You got to hit him, you got to bruise him, you got to break his arm, his leg, his ribs — you got to cut him, spike him, you got to smell his blood, you got to *put your spikes in his chest!* You got to *score!*
MR. COBB. Stealing home. The most audacious move in baseball.

TY. The complete destruction of the opposing team's ability to protect itself. And nobody did it better than me. *(A projection quickly appears. It is the famous photograph of Cobb spiking a catcher in a play at the plate. Cobb is fully a foot in the air, his foot planted deeply in the catcher's stomach.)*
PEACH. Now *that* is a trip around the bases. You can bet Babe Ruth never took that trip. Or ever could. I could hit home runs. I hit five in two games once. But he could never move around the bases like me. *(Lights quickly down on all three. The projection fades out much slower. As soon as it is gone, lights fade up on Peach, lying face up on the bench we saw early in the play. His shirt is off, and his face has a pained expression. Charleston sits on a low stool behind the bench, watching him. Charleston wears the uniform of the Homestead Grays. The word "GRAYS" appears in block print across his chest.)*
CHARLESTON. How you feeling?
PEACH. What's it to you?
CHARLESTON. Just curious, that's all. That was a fine talk you gave about Babe Ruth just now.
PEACH. It was not about Babe Ruth. It was about me. *(Peach lifts up as he speaks. It is painful.)* Ow! *(Peach reaches towards his right leg, but it's too sore to touch.)*
CHARLESTON. What's bothering you there? What pain you got there?
PEACH. Nothin'.
CHARLESTON. Something's bothering you.
PEACH. It's nothin'. Just a strawberry. From slidin', that's all.
CHARLESTON. I used to get those. Rip your whole leg up, sliding into a base. All the way from knee to hip. Fields we played on, we were lucky to have any skin left at all by season's end. How bad's the one you got?
PEACH. Bad. Sometimes it don't hurt so much. Sometimes...
CHARLESTON. You don't have to have it, you know.
PEACH. What?
CHARLESTON. You don't have to have it. You can just let it go, now. *(A beat.)*
PEACH. *(Quietly.)* I want it.
CHARLESTON. *(Nodding.)* Yup. You and me sure did get

around the bases different from the Babe.
PEACH. What do you know about it?
CHARLESTON. Plenty. We had us a Babe Ruth. "The Black Babe Ruth," they called him. Name was Josh Gibson. You remember him. I'm proud to say I played with Josh — managed him too. That man hit the ball farther than anybody I ever seen, including Ruth. We had a Black Lou Gehrig, too: Buck Leonard. And John Henry Lloyd — he was the Black Honus Wagner. Me, I was the Black Cobb. We didn't get to pick who they compared us to, you understand. Just the man in the white leagues you played the most like. Your position, your ability, your temper.
PEACH. My temper?
CHARLESTON. I was a fighter, same as you. Joined the Army when I was 15. Fought my way through that, then fought my way through baseball. Joined my hometown club, the Indianapolis ABC's. Used to spike a lot of players. Why there was men wouldn't even try to tag me. They'd just step back and let me steal the base. I fought folks all the time. Wasn't just players, neither. I fought umps — hell, one time I punched an owner in the face. On the field, off the field — didn't care where I fought. I hit a man in the shower once, just for throwing a bad pitch in a game. Toughness — that's why I got the name the Black Cobb. That, and hitting over .400 most of the time. It wasn't the worst title, I suppose. It was the only way white folks knew me. They never remembered no Oscar Charleston. Just the Black Cobb. Kind of strange, having your fame with another man's name on it. *(A beat.)* You feeling comfortable? You resting easy now?
PEACH. Get outta here.
CHARLESTON. *(Smiles.)* I would if I could. I'd leave you all to yourself. Don't seem to be able to, though. It's like you pull me to you. Wherever you are, I got to be. Feels like you're calling me, all the time.
PEACH. I'm not callin' you.
CHARLESTON. Something is.
PEACH. Somethin's callin' me too, but I don't go round botherin' other people about it! *(Peach tries to sit up, falls back in*

pain.) Go on — get away from me.
CHARLESTON. Can't get away.
PEACH. Then get back! As far as you can.
CHARLESTON. Sure that's what you want? *(Peach is silent. Charleston rises, moves toward the darkness.)* Can't go far. Maybe just out of sight. *(Charleston disappears into the shadows. We hear his voice from off.)* How's this?
PEACH. Better. *(Lights fade out on Peach, come up on Mr. Cobb and Ty.)*
MR. COBB. When I was 21, I married a woman named Charlie.
TY. No cracks!
MR. COBB. We had five children. I was a family man — good one, too.
TY. We didn't get divorced 'til every one of those kids was grown.
MR. COBB. *(With a disapproving look at Ty.)* It's true we had our problems, but we also had a sense of decency. I didn't chase after women like a lot of ballplayers. I slept with a gun — not other women. It was a hell of a lot safer.
TY. Once I retired, I was home a lot more. After awhile, things got unpleasant.
MR. COBB. My marriage was no worse than anyone else's.
TY. *(To audience.)* How do you make a wife love you? How do you do that?
MR. COBB. Charlie loved me!
TY. Always? *(To audience.)* Marriage was created so even the greatest of men would have the opportunity to fail.
MR. COBB. I did not fail with her! I ... I —
TY. I what? *(Lights up quickly on Peach.)*
PEACH. I loved her when we married. She was barely 17. Somethin' happens when you're in love. You lose all sense of how to do things. I left the Tigers in the middle of a pennant race to marry Charlie. Took the train all the way down to Georgia — three-day trip. Got to Charlie's folks' house one minute before the ceremony. And there she was — standin' there in lace and flowers, lookin' like the answer to every question that had ever been asked. The local paper said our wed-

din' was "marked by that simplicity which is the key-note of excellence." I thought the fans were gonna be mad when we got back. They weren't, though. They stood and cheered. *(Smiling at the recollection.)* The next two weeks, my battin' average slipped 20 points. I can't tell you what sweetness it was bein' with her back then, startin' out. Still sometimes I think I knew even then, right in the middle of all that first pleasure, that it would die.

MR. COBB. There's no hope in life. When you're young, you do things by instinct, blind. Other people get married, you get married. Other people have children —

TY. By the time you know what you're doing, you've already done it. Wrong. *(As lights fade out on Peach.)* There is no feeling that compares with living in a dead marriage.

MR. COBB. *(With distaste.)* Years of endless ... companionship.

TY. Watchin' her turn the children against me. My oldest son liked tennis, for God's sake. Tennis! Tyrus Raymond Cobb, Junior. And he hated baseball.

MR. COBB. He didn't hate it. He just had trouble with —

TY. He had trouble with everything. He flopped around in school for years. Flunked out of Princeton, flunked out of Yale. Didn't get a profession until he was over thirty. Then look what he became: a gynecologist.

MR. COBB. The son of Ty Cobb. A gynecologist. Try telling that to your friends at an oldtimers game.

TY. I barely spoke to him for 15 years. My own son.

MR. COBB. Let it go.

TY. Charlie made him like that. My wife encouraged every lazy, self-interested urge he had —

MR. COBB. Let it go! *(To audience.)* When he was 42, he died. Brain cancer. Near the end, I made up with him. He left a wife and three children. I used to visit them.

TY. My younger son Herschel died the year before. Heart attack.

MR. COBB. Two sons in two years. Great lives suffer great tragedies.

TY. So do common ones.

MR. COBB. *What the hell use is a family if it falls apart on you!?*

I put 39 years into that marriage, and every one of my children sided with their mother. Where's the justice in that? Eh? What league did she ever lead in hitting? When'd she ever make a million bucks?
TY. In the divorce, that's when.
MR. COBB. We divorced in 1947. Charlie hired some young sonofabitch lawyer named Melvin Belli to claim I was worth 14 million.
TY. It was a damn lie. I wasn't that rich. We settled out of court. Terms of the agreement were never revealed. Ever. To anyone. So you can all take your curiosity and — *(Lights up quickly on Peach.)*
PEACH. God, I loved her! She had hazel eyes. She was a Southern lady.
TY. *(As lights fade on Peach.)* When we were through, I was calling her, "that old woman."
MR. COBB. Great lives suffer great tragedies. *(Mr. Cobb and Ty start out. Charleston enters before Ty can exit. Ty turns and watches as Charleston, now in the uniform of a Cuban team — Santa Clara — does warm-up exercises.)*
CHARLESTON. *(Continuing to exercise.)* Hey, there. Good to see you.
TY. What are you doing?
CHARLESTON. Me? Getting ready for some Cuban ball. Used to go down there all the time. Make some winter money, enjoy the sunshine. Not a bad life. Lots of players used to do that, black and white.
TY. Not me.
CHARLESTON. Not ever?
TY. Nope.
CHARLESTON. That ain't what I heard. I heard the Tigers went down there in 1910. You were with 'em.
TY. Doesn't mean I played.
CHARLESTON. Oh, you played. I heard it from John Henry Lloyd and Bruce Petway both, and they was there. You played against Cubans and American blacks. 1910. Five games.
TY. What the hell's it matter if I did?
CHARLESTON. Don't matter at all. Heard you hit real well

in those games. Almost .400, something like that.

TY. Probably. I don't recall.

CHARLESTON. Tell me — how come you never played against black players again? *(Ty is silent.)* Is it 'cause Bruce Petway threw you out trying to steal second?

(Ty regards him grimly. Charleston goes on stretching.) That's what Bruce always figured. Figured getting thrown out by a black catcher like him bothered you something awful. Shouldn't have. Bruce was a fine catcher. He threw us all out, one time or another. *(Ty is silent. Charleston speaks in a sincere tone.)* Sure wish I could've played against you. Even just one time. That would've been an honor. I'd have enjoyed that.

TY. Could we change the subject?

CHARLESTON. 'Course we can. I didn't mean to keep going on. It was just such good money down there in Cuba. I'm surprised you passed it up.

TY. I was not responsible for the color bar in baseball!!

CHARLESTON. I never said you were.

TY. *You're here, aren't you!?* Coloreds were forced out of the major leagues before I was born! If you want to go haunt somebody, go haunt Cap Anson. Go haunt Spalding, Comiskey, Landis — all of 'em. *They* made the decisions, not me. There is a time and place for everything. The place for you was Brooklyn. The time was 1947. It's as simple as that. *(Charleston stands, takes a last stretch.)*

CHARLESTON. Maybe you're right. Only problem is, I stopped playing in 1937. *(He stares at Ty.)* To play against you, just once. Would've been an honor. *(Charleston exits into the darkness.)*

TY. *(Calling after him.)* I never objected to coloreds playing! You hear me?! Never! I was exactly like everybody else! *(Ty continues to stare off after Charleston. Peach and Mr. Cobb enter. They look at Ty, as if they expect him to join them, but Ty is oblivious.)*

MR. COBB. *(To audience.)* I played in three World Series in my life.

PEACH. Three World Series in a row, actually, and... *(Peach looks at Ty, waiting for him to speak. Ty continues to stare off, Peach tries cueing him again.)* And... *(A beat.)* And...

TY. *(Finally looking around.)* What? Oh ... and we lost all three. *(Ty looks off again.)*
MR. COBB. I don't deny it.
PEACH. Besides, you could look it up.
MR. COBB. Well, so what? So we lost. Lots of great players never even saw a World Series. I got there three times.
PEACH. And lost.
MR. COBB. We had a good team, but always went flat at the finish.
TY. The Tigers — my Tigers — lost three World Series in three consecutive years.
PEACH. The only team ever to do that.
MR. COBB. It was a failure.
PEACH. Losin' three World Series.
MR. COBB. Well, good. I admitted it. Let's go on.
PEACH. *(To audience, his mood unbroken.)* When I first told my father I wanted to be a ballplayer, it was like tellin' him I wanted to be a vagrant.
MR. COBB. What are you talking about now?
PEACH. We argued over it for a long time. But then I had a chance to play for a team over in Alabama — semi-pro, they hardly paid you nothin'. And he let me go. All my life he'd been like a glass mountain — you couldn't climb him. Always sayin' no, demandin' more. And then there he was, suddenly. Sayin', "Go on — go to Alabama, try baseball." For him it must've been like sayin', "Go try a life of crime."
TY. He said one more thing, too. He said, "Don't come home a failure."
MR. COBB. That's not important.
TY. Hell, it ain't!
PEACH. He was dead before he knew if I was a failure or not. He wasn't dead in me, though. You know, I might've been a .280 hitter if he hadn't said that to me. It's easy enough — just let your concentration slip. As it was, I hit .367 for my career. Over 24 years. .367.
MR. COBB. *(Seizing on it, cheerfully.)* That's the highest of anybody — by far — ever.
TY. "Don't come home a failure."

PEACH. Most hits, most runs scored, most stolen bases — season, most stolen bases — career, most singles, most triples. Records I held for 50 years — longer, some of 'em. Most records.
MR. COBB. *(As before.)* At one time, I held ninety records. Ninety!
TY. Don't come home a failure.
MR. COBB. Shut the hell up!
PEACH. I had to get every hit I could. I had to steal every base.
TY. How do you please a dead man?
MR. COBB. It wasn't a matter of that.
PEACH. How could I take any joke lightly? Those men knew I wanted their job. They knew I was goin' to get it. There was no joke.
TY. I roomed alone on the road. I never was alone, though.
PEACH. Don't come home a failure.
TY. My father shouldn't have come home at all, one night.
MR. COBB. GET OUT OF HERE! NOW! GET OUT! *(A beat. Ty and Peach make no move to leave. Mr. Cobb regards the audience with embarrassment.)* I competed over everything in life. It's true. Over matters of no importance. I once played a golf match against Babe Ruth — Bette Davis presented the award — and I treated it like the World Series. I hated myself like that. Couldn't stand myself. But I never, never changed.
PEACH. I thought as I grew older I'd become — you know — wiser and kinder? I didn't, though. I just found myself developin' more and more into ... myself. *(A beat. They stare off in different directions.)*
MR. COBB. You see what happens when you don't let me choose the topic of conversation? I mean, this is ridiculous. Why should I be depressed, after what I've done in life? Hell, I've done so much, I can't — *(To audience.)* Who was the first professional athlete in America to star in a feature motion picture?
TY. *(Turning away disgustedly.)* Oh, God.
MR. COBB. That's right — me. In 1916, I had the lead in a movie written by Grantland Rice. *(Looking at Peach.)* It was

called ... *(Peach hesitates.)* Come on, it was called ...
PEACH. *(Warming to it.)* It was called *Somewhere In Georgia,* and it was about a young Georgia ballplayer who played for the Detroit Tigers.
MR. COBB. You could say it was tailored for me.
TY. I'm leaving.
MR. COBB. Leaving?
TY. Let me know when you're remembering a fight. *(Ty starts to exit. Mr. Cobb blocks his way.)*
MR. COBB. Wait a minute! Wait, now! This is important. This is — this is my festive side! *(Unwillingly, Ty remains. Mr. Cobb speaks to the audience.)* I'd acted before, you know. I toured on the living stage, as Billy Bolton the handsome halfback in a play called *The College Widow.*
PEACH. Lots of ballplayers acted in Vaudeville in the off-season, but I held out for a real character in a real play. It paid better.
MR. COBB. I got good reviews — especially in the South, where it counted. Oh, one sonofabitch in Birmingham criticized me, but I fixed him. Sent him all my good reviews plus a note.
PEACH. "I am a better actor than you are, a better drama critic than you are, I make more money than you do, and I know I am a better ballplayer — so why should inferiors criticize superiors?" That's what I wrote him. He probably still feels terrible.
TY. I should've killed him.
MR. COBB. That's enough!
TY. Hell, it is! That's the whole problem with this country. We hold things in too much. We should let 'em out, fight when we have to.
MR. COBB. We can't always —
TY. These are some of my fights.
MR. COBB. No fights —
TY. I beat up an umpire under the grandstand. That one's a lie, but I'll claim it anyway.
MR. COBB. I told you —
PEACH. Nearly fought Ruth once, in 1924. Took both teams

to keep us apart.
MR. COBB. *(Starting out.)* I'm going.
TY. Pulled a gun on my butcher —
MR. COBB. *(Returning.) I did no such —*
PEACH. Threw my bat in the stands once, protestin' a call.
MR. COBB. Never!
PEACH. Didn't hit nobody.
MR. COBB. Can't you see what this does?! How do you want to be remembered?
TY. As dangerous.
PEACH. As alive. *(Charleston enters. He wears streetclothes, circa 1950.)*
CHARLESTON. June, 1908. *(They turn and look at him.)*
MR. COBB. *(To Ty and Peach.)* Now look what you've done.
CHARLESTON. June, 1908. Fred Collins. Black streetworker. You stepped in some asphalt he was laying down. He yelled at you. You hit him and knocked him down.
MR. COBB. Why should I want to remember that one?
CHARLESTON. Oh — I'm sorry. Thought you did. I'll go. *(He starts out again.)*
TY. Besides, I barely touched him.
CHARLESTON. *(Stopping, looking around.)* He filed charges.
MR. COBB. *(To Ty.)* Let it be, will you? *(To Charleston.)* You just go on. If I hit him, I hit him. No need to remember it. *(Charleston starts out again.)*
TY. If he'd been white, he'd have been honored I touched him at all.
MR. COBB. *(To Ty.)* Will you just — !?
TY. *(To Peach, as Charleston stops again.)* Couldn't believe it when the judge found me guilty.
PEACH. He suspended the sentence, though.
TY. Even he could tell a rich man from a poor man.
CHARLESTON. You still had to pay 75 bucks.
TY. *(Aggressively, to Charleston.)* Yeah, and I miss it to this day!
MR. COBB. *(Trying to usher Charleston out.)* No need to go into all this. It was an isolated incident.
CHARLESTON. *(Sliding away from Mr. Cobb.)* September, 1909.
TY. What's wrong with that one?

CHARLESTON. Nothing. You got in a fight with a night watchman in Cleveland, that's all.
TY. And he was colored. What do you want to make of it?!
MR. COBB. Nothing. He doesn't want to make anything of it.
PEACH. George Stansfield. I remember him. He pulled a club on me.
CHARLESTON. You pulled a knife on him.
PEACH. He pulled a gun on me!
CHARLESTON. You cut him.
TY. And I'd do it again. He practically killed me with that club.
CHARLESTON. It was you got convicted. *(Ty goes for Charleston. Mr. Cobb and Peach grab Ty before he can reach him. Charleston stands alert but calm.)*
TY. Goddammit, I'll —
MR. COBB. Stop it!
TY. *(Struggling to get loose.)* You've got no right! You hear me?! You've got no right to throw my life up to me! I'm Ty Cobb!
MR. COBB. Let it go — !
TY. TYRUS RAYMOND COBB!! I had fights!
MR. COBB. *(To Charleston, as he helps hold Ty.)* I was drunk those times —
TY. I was stone-cold *sober!!* *(On "sober" Ty breaks free. He confronts Charleston, who hasn't moved.)* If I fought coloreds with my fists, I was only doing what other whites did in other ways. The country I grew up in hated coloreds. It hated 'em, it by God feared 'em and it still does! Don't you point me up as some kind of special person on that score — I wasn't!
CHARLESTON. *(Quietly.)* You're right. There's nothing special about you.
TY. *(Starting for him again.)* You know what I mean! *(Peach moves Ty away from Charleston.)*
MR. COBB. Assault and battery. That's what it was, all right. They fined me $100 and costs. I tell you, the courts of Ohio have degenerated sharply. You know I helped colored folks too, now and then. *(Charleston laughs.)* I did. Built housing for 'em down in Georgia. Wasn't charity — I made money on it — but

I built for 'em all the same.
PEACH. We had a colored mascot on the team — you know, a batboy. One winter I gave him a job at my car dealership in Augusta, cleaning or something.
TY. *(Forcefully.)* In my life I was never greatly criticized for my attitude towards the colored — except by colored newspapers, and they were biased.
MR. COBB. Let's not fight. Just once, let's not. *(With a disgusted look, Ty moves away.)*
CHARLESTON. It's hard to be the best at something. Gives you a nervous feeling. Like there's no one left to fight against — no way to get any better, as good as you can be, as you *need* to be. The world almost fails a man like that. Nothing in the world can beat him. Nothing but time.
TY. I'll beat time!
CHARLESTON. *(Shaking his head, smiling.)* You sure do try. *(Charleston exits silently.)*
MR. COBB. He's right.
TY. What do you mean, he's right?
MR. COBB. He's right. What chance is there against time? Eats you up whole. Forty-two years old, and I was finished. What good was I to anyone when I retired?
TY. What good? I hit .323 my last year. Could've gone on forever. I had plenty of fight left in me. Still do.
MR. COBB. That's the problem.
TY. My God. Sometimes I can't believe how old I got. *(Ty exits. Mr. Cobb and Peach exchange a look, then Peach exits.)*
MR. COBB. I was forty-two when I left baseball. I spent the next thirty-three years of my life as someone who couldn't do the one thing that made him special. I could get richer, I could hunt, I could have children I didn't understand, a wife who loved me less and less. I could go to oldtimers games, dinners, give interviews. But I could never again ... feel triumph. My wife Charlie and I bought a retirement home in Atherton, California. We lived there fifteen years, during which she filed four divorce suits. The last one took. The place had seven bedrooms, swimming pool, guest house, servants' quarters, grounds — God, I hated it. Once she was gone, I didn't know what I

was supposed to do with myself. I fished, hunted, made more money, gambled, wrote condescending articles about baseball today, got drunk and insulted people, kept a sonofabitch list, sued people, sat, stared.... When my cancer came, the only thing that would keep the pain down was a 50% solution of Jack Daniels and milk. And that was me at the end — a sick man shambling around in his robe all day, drinking that. Loneliness is the main road in life — the rest is just a detour. Hell, loneliness isn't even the road. It's the land itself. This country was built on loneliness. It is loneliness. *(Lights fade up on Ty.)*
TY. I think married people should only see each other occasionally. Meet at weddings, funerals that sort of thing. Men and women don't like living the same way. Why should they pretend they do? *(Lights fade up on Peach.)*
PEACH. We should all live alone, and only meet once in awhile in the dark. Then at least we'd have an excuse for lyin' there, wonderin' who the hell this was next to us. *(Peach exits. Mr. Cobb opens a wooden folding chair and sits in it.)*
MR. COBB. The proudest day of my life — and the saddest day of my life — was the day I was inducted into the Baseball Hall of Fame. I was there the day the place opened. First man ever voted in. I out-polled Babe Ruth, Honus Wagner, Cy Young, Walter Johnson, Christy Mathewson, Tris Speaker, Nap Lajoie, Wee Willie Keeler, George Sisler, Eddie Collins and Grover Cleveland Alexander. *(Projection fades up. It is the formal portrait of the above men at the 1939 inaugural induction ceremony at Cooperstown. TY opens another folding chair and sits next to Mr. Cobb.)*
TY. No man who'd ever played got more votes than me. We were all there, too — the ones still living. Plus Connie Mack. We'd been the greatest in the game. Now we were a bunch of old men sitting in folding chairs. Something horrifying about seeing athletes you knew 30 years ago all wasted away. Like having a dozen mirrors around you.
MR. COBB. But the mirrors are all you have left, so you go. Summer after summer, you go back to that ceremony in Cooperstown. You eat the banquet.
TY. You drink, you visit with men who grow older and older.

MR. COBB. You sit in the folding chairs.
TY. The greatest players of our time. Out of time.
MR. COBB. You drink a little more. You tell the worn-out stories.
TY. You drink a little more.
MR. COBB. You let the night steal over. People leave all around you.
TY. You don't even notice that you're last. Talking with one other man — maybe a young man, someone who works there. Someone assigned to see that you're all right.
MR. COBB. Someone who helps you up the street, teetering — more from drink than age — under the stars, in the cool summer night, to your hotel.
TY. And you think, this moment —
MR. COBB. Is the purest heaven —
TY. And the purest hell —
MR. COBB. I will ever know. *(The projection slowly fades. Lights crossfade to Peach, now wearing a suit, circa 1910.)*
PEACH. People say I was the most intelligent player in the game. But I felt things, too. Whenever I walked into a ballpark, it was like fallin' in love for the first time — again and again. As though you could do that. And the feel of the glove and the bat — these objects that were always there, between you and the other man. They were tools you used, but they were also a part of your body. They made me feel more natural, more physically complete. It's time's fault — not mine — that I traded them for a Luger and a bagful of money.
TY. *(Moving into the light downstage, as lights fade on Peach.)* Dammit, that's enough. To hell with all this moaning. So what if I had it bad at the end? Who doesn't? We all break down. What we do *before* — that's the point. I did more'n anybody. Hell, I played poker with Presidents. Don't you dream of pitying me. *(The projection of Babe Ruth fades up again. Ty looks around at it.)* What's that doing there!? Get rid of that! Get *rid* of it! *(The projection doesn't fade. Ty shouts at it.)* You fat sonofabitch! You couldn't touch me, you hear!? You were no damn match! You wouldn't have lasted one night in the Hotel Pontchartrain, I'll tell you that! *(The projection crossfades into a*

picture of the Hotel Pontchartrain in Detroit. Ty turns to the audience.) The Hotel Pontchartrain, in Detroit. Or the Oak Bar in the Hotel Pontchartrain. That's where I went — the Oak Bar. Not to drink, to listen. Certain rich and powerful men came to that bar. Men with names like Olds, Packard, Chevrolet. The Stanley Steamer twins. Men who ran Hudson, Hupmobile, Dodge. No city in America boomed the way Detroit did in those years. The entire automobile industry was growing up like some enormous baby — utterly selfish, utterly determined. Deals flew around that room. Tips. All you had to do was sit at the end of the bar and listen. They *told* you what to do. Where were all my teammates then, eh? Where were the know-it-all sportswriters? Down the street in some newspaper bar, getting stiff. While I was getting rich. By listening — by using the same brain I used on the field. That's why I'm special. It's the money I made! The way I made it! It's my brain! My instinct to dominate and destroy those around me. *(Charleston crosses past Ty. Ty looks at him nervously, then to audience.)* I was just like everybody else!! *(Lights snap out on Ty. Lights fade up on Mr. Cobb, alone.)*

MR. COBB. Babe Ruth wouldn't have known how to use the Oak Bar at the Hotel Pontchartrain. Hell, he would've ended up *under* it. Ruth was a freak. He was an egg on stilts. You loved him, though. Late in life I sometimes drove by Ruth's old apartment on Riverside Drive in New York. I used to go up there after games, when we played the Yankees. Ruth and I would sit for hours and talk. He'd eat about half a dozen sandwiches and smoke a cigar. The sun would set over the Hudson. He'd chomp away, talk with me like I was his best friend. I never saw a man who looked so much like he belonged in the world. *(Lights crossfade to Charleston sitting on a folding chair. He wears the uniform of the 1936 Pittsburgh Crawfords. Peach enters with a folding chair, seems surprised to see Charleston. Peach grudgingly sits next to him.)*

CHARLESTON. I'm in the Hall of Fame, you know. They let me in.

PEACH. When?

CHARLESTON. 1976. Years after I died. They slipped me in

with five white boys. Robin Roberts, Bob Lemon — good players. 1976. Not many folks knew who I was by then. "Oscar Charleston? Who the hell was he?" Not too many stop by my plaque. They're always over there by your plaque, or Ruth's, or Aaron's.
PEACH. What did they put on your plaque?
CHARLESTON. Why do you want to know?
PEACH. No reason.
CHARLESTON. You afraid they put "The Black Cobb" on there?
PEACH. *(He is.)* No, it's just —
CHARLESTON. Relax — they didn't. We can both relax on that one. On my plaque they said I was versatile. They said I "hit well over .300 most years." Most years. Like saying Joe Louis was a pretty good fighter. It's all they got, though. Nobody kept records much where I played. Just a few newspaper clippings, box scores. Most of them are lost. No numbers for me. No proof of what I did. Just people's memory. They're mostly dead. Soon they all will be. No one living will have ever seen me play. *(A beat.)*
PEACH. What, um ... what uniform is that?
CHARLESTON. This is the Pittsburgh Crawfords.
PEACH. What's a Crawford?
CHARLESTON. Show respect. This was a great team.
PEACH. You play on a lot of teams?
CHARLESTON. Chicago American Giants, Philadelphia Hilldales, Pittsburgh Crawfords, Indianapolis ABC's, Harrisburg Giants, Detroit Stars and the Homestead Grays. Plus a few Cuban teams.
PEACH. You must've been good. Everybody wanted to keep you so bad.
CHARLESTON. I had to play wherever a team had money. Most of us changed 'round quite a bit. Didn't matter, though. We knew who we were. We knew how good we were. The best ever to play the game.
PEACH. Damn it — quit sayin' that! There's no comparison, and you know it!
CHARLESTON. There ain't? What's the best team you ever

played on?
PEACH. Best team?
CHARLESTON. Most successful. What year?
PEACH. 1908 Tigers, I suppose. No — 1909.
CHARLESTON. Who were the stars that year? Tell the names.
PEACH. The stars? Me ... um, Wahoo Sam Crawford —
CHARLESTON. "Wahoo?" *(Charleston shakes his head derisively.)*
PEACH. Davy Jones —
CHARLESTON. Fishbait.
PEACH. Donie Bush —
CHARLESTON. Bush-league.
PEACH. George Mullin.
CHARLESTON. Nothin'.
PEACH. How would you know — !?
CHARLESTON. My best team was the 1932 Crawfords. Player for player we got you whipped. We had Josh Gibson, Cool Papa Bell, Judy Johnson, Satchel Paige and me. There's five right there that's in the Hall of Fame. How many from that Tiger team of yours? Two? Sometimes I think the major leagues would've been a step down from where I played.
PEACH. It's that name they put on you, isn't it? The Black Cobb. You got that, you started thinkin' all sorts of things.
CHARLESTON. I don't need a name to know how good I was. Don't need people to call me the Black Cobb or not — no more than you need me to call you the White Charleston.
PEACH. You sonofabitch!
CHARLESTON. Oh, I made the list now, huh?
PEACH. What is it you want!? Why don't you get the hell out of my dream!?
CHARLESTON. Maybe it ain't just your dream! *(A beat.)* You want to know what I want? I want to see the part of your mind that felt happy the first time you heard about the Black Cobb. That felt lucky — that was glad it wasn't you, that you weren't the black man, the Black Cobb, all tucked away out of sight in the Negro Leagues. I want to see the part of your mind that felt — *fine* — right then. I want to hold that in my hand, and look at it. I want to see what kind of thing that is.
PEACH. Look at yourself. You felt the same thing. Every time

you saw an average ballplayer. Every time you swung a bat. "Thank God I'm me. Thank God I got a built-in advantage." Everybody presses whatever advantage they got. You're no different. You're the same as me.
CHARLESTON. Nice to hear you say it.
PEACH. *(As Mr. Cobb enters.)* You know what I mean!!
CHARLESTON. Better'n you do. But you and me, we played against those average ballplayers. They got the same chance we did, on the same field. You never gave me that chance.
MR. COBB. When could I have played you?
CHARLESTON. 1915, 1922 and 1923. Three different years the Tigers — your Tigers — played exhibition games against teams I played on. Three different chances — three different Octobers. You could've been there, and you never were. When you did that, you cheated yourself out of something for all time.
PEACH. I never cheated myself out of nothin'.
CHARLESTON. Out of the chance to know. You'll never know if you were better. All the statistics, the numbers, the fame — they'll never tell you. You had the chance to play me and you never did. You'll never be able to say, "I played Oscar Charleston. I played the Black Cobb. And I was better."
PEACH. You sonofabitch!
CHARLESTON. *(Laughs.)* That's right, I'm a sonofabitch!
PEACH. You *are* a sonofabitch!
CHARLESTON. A sonofabitch, I don't deny it!
PEACH. Son-of-a-bitch!
CHARLESTON. Say it again.
PEACH. Sonofabitch.
CHARLESTON. Say it forever. All you had to do was play me once — I would've left you alone. Now I'll be with you forever.
PEACH. Sonofa*bitch!*
CHARLESTON. And say goodbye to your record book, too. Without us in your league, the record book doesn't exist.
PEACH. SONOFABITCH!!
CHARLESTON. Again!
PEACH. Sonofabitch!

CHARLESTON. Again.
PEACH. Sonofa — *(He stops suddenly, mouth open.)*
CHARLESTON. Come on, again! Again! How many times you said it, you reckon, in your life? You're so tired of saying it, you can't get the word out of your mouth. *It's the same for me.* Life's full of sonsofbitches — you know the biggest sonofabitch of all? When it disappears! What you said, what you did, people you loved, people you hated — when it wears out, fades away. Places you played, the times you lived in — things you had a right to! That happened to you the day you died — or maybe even the last day you put on a uniform. It happened to me the first day. The first time I ever walked onto a field, or put my hand in a glove or held a bat. Everything was there for me, and nothing was there. You worry about being erased? You should've been me. I was alive and dead at the same time. *(A beat.)* You don't mean a damn to me. You been swallowed up, along with everything else. You leave no mark. You think anger can save you? You don't know what anger is. *(Charleston picks up his chair, folds it.)* They put me in the Hall of Fame in 1976. Forgot me the minute my plaque was on the wall. *(Charleston exits. They watch him go.)*
MR. COBB. We should never have spoken to him. That's how trouble always comes: from going where there's no reason to go.
PEACH. *(To audience.)* November, 1896. In the Fifth Grade, I beat up a fat boy. See, he missed a word in a spelling contest. Made us boys lose to the girls. I had to beat him up. It was my first fight that I remember — real one anyway, with blood. The way that first punch I connected with made me feel. Pleasure and terror all at once. The kids all screamed. Surrounded by screamin' kids. In the eye of the storm. A storm I could create myself anytime, out of pure need. Out of pure need. *(Ty enters. Over his shoulder are a pair of baseball shoes.)*
TY. When they opened the Hall of Fame in 1939, the first thing they put in it was a pair of shoes. My shoes. My spikes. The first symbol of baseball to enter that building. They didn't have to choose 'em. Babe Ruth had plenty of stuff lying around. But they chose my spikes. That's because they truly

knew the game.

MR. COBB. What's it matter? Ruth *was* the game. You should've seen people when Babe Ruth died. Sure he died young, but still.

PEACH. Whole city of New York wept. Whole nation.

MR. COBB. When I went, I just ... went. *(Projection: the Cobb mausoleum in Royston, Georgia.)*

TY. Article in the *Times*. Cobb? Was he still alive?

MR. COBB. Good myth should go out with more than that.

PEACH. Ty Cobb died of cancer in a hospital when he was old and unconscious.

MR. COBB. I'd been a part of baseball for over fifty years, but only two major leaguers came to my funeral. The town had to get a bunch of Little-Leaguers to line the way. Shit.

TY. The most hated man in baseball.

PEACH. My father died better than me.

MR. COBB. I'll never make a myth.

TY. I was too real for myths. You couldn't sell what I was. *(The projection fades. Gently, TY sets the spikes down before him. All three men look at them.)* I'm buried in Georgia, but this is where I really lie. First thing that went inside the Hall. Not a bat, not a ball. My spikes. I've put my spikes somewhere else, too. In you. In every one of you. *(Ty exits. Peach and Mr. Cobb look at each other.)*

PEACH. *(To audience.)* You ever hear of Germany Schaefer? He was a Tiger. Way back — My God, I don't remember anymore — back when I was startin' out. He once did somethin' on a ballfield I never did understand. He stole first base. That's right. He was standin' on second, and he suddenly just let out a whoop and stole first. Pitcher was too amazed to even make a throw. I always thought Germany did it to drive the opposition crazy. You know, make 'em not know what was comin' at 'em next. *(With an endless puzzlement.)* That's not why he did it, though. It was for love. He just ... loved the game. *(A beat.)* Strangest thing I ever saw. *(Peach exits.)*

MR. COBB. *(To audience.)* I built a hospital, I created the Cobb Educational Fund, I provided for my heirs better than most men could dream. Once I was gone, my home town of Royston built a Ty Cobb Museum. They were going to have a bronze statue of me too, but they had to cancel that for lack of funds. The museum itself closed eventually, for lack of visitors. *(Charleston enters and stands silently, in the Homestead Grays uniform. Mr. Cobb notices, keeps speaking to audience.)* No man wants to be forgotten. Every man, if he breathed, wants someone to remember that fact. No shame in it, a perfectly human ... aspiration. I was the quickest, meanest, smartest, fiercest ... best ... man ever to play the game. *(With a second short look at Charleston, then back to the audience.)* Just ... remember. *(Mr. Cobb exits as lights fade down to a pin spot on the spikes, then to black.)*

THE END

PROPERTY LIST

Baseball (Mr. Cobb)
Writing utensil (Mr. Cobb)
3-4 baseball bats (Peach)
Brown paper bag
Luger pistol (Mr. Cobb)
Big-game rifle (Ty)
Pistol (1906) (Peach)
Dry mop (Charleston)
Stool (Charleston)
Wooden folding chair (Mr. Cobb)
Wooden folding chair (Ty)
Folding chair (Charleston)
Folding chair (Peach)
Baseball shoes with spikes (Ty)

COSTUME LIST

Robe (Mr. Cobb)
Socks (Peach)
Red baseball uniform pants and shirt (Peach)
Business suit (1930s) (Ty)
Indianapolis ABCs 1921 baseball uniform (white) Charleston
Detroit Tigers baseball uniform (Peach)
Hunting garb (1930s, North American) (Ty)
Homestead Grays baseball uniform (Charleston)
Baseball uniform of Cuban team from Santa Clara (Charleston)
Street clothes (1950) (Charleston)
Suit (1910) (Peach)
Pittsburgh Crawfords 1936 baseball uniform (Charleston)

TODAY'S HOTTEST NEW PLAYS

❏ **THREE VIEWINGS by Jeffrey Hatcher.** Three comic-dramatic monologues, set in a midwestern funeral parlor, interweave as they explore the ways we grieve, remember, and move on. *"Finally, what we have been waiting for: a new, true, idiosyncratic voice in the theater. And don't tell me you hate monologues; you can't hate them more than I do. But these are much more: windows into the deep of each speaker's fascinating, paradoxical, unique soul, and windows out into a gallery of surrounding people, into hilarious and horrific coincidences and conjunctions, into the whole dirty but irresistible business of living in this damnable but spellbinding place we presume to call the world."* - *New York Magazine.* [1M, 2W]

❏ **HAVING OUR SAY by Emily Mann.** The Delany Sisters' Bestselling Memoir is now one of Broadway's Best-Loved Plays! Having lived over one hundred years apiece, Bessie and Sadie Delany have plenty to say, and their story is not simply African-American history or women's history...it is our history as a nation. *"The most provocative and entertaining family play to reach Broadway in a long time."* - *New York Times.* *"Fascinating, marvelous, moving and forceful."* - *Associated Press.* [2W]

❏ **THE YOUNG MAN FROM ATLANTA Winner of the 1995 Pulitzer Prize. by Horton Foote.** An older couple attempts to recover from the suicide death of their only son, but the menacing truth of why he died, and what a certain Young Man from Atlanta had to do with it, keeps them from the peace they so desperately need. *"Foote ladles on character and period nuances with a density unparalleled in any living playwright."* - *NY Newsday.* [5M, 4W]

❏ **SIMPATICO by Sam Shepard.** Years ago, two men organized a horse racing scam. Now, years later, the plot backfires against the ringleader when his partner decides to come out of hiding. *"Mr. Shepard writing at his distinctive, savage best."* - *New York Times.* [3M, 3W]

❏ **MOONLIGHT by Harold Pinter.** The love-hate relationship between a dying man and his family is the subject of Harold Pinter's first full-length play since *Betrayal*. *"Pinter works the language as a master pianist works the keyboard."* - *New York Post.* [4M, 2W, 1G]

❏ **SYLVIA by A.R. Gurney.** This romantic comedy, the funniest to come along in years, tells the story of a twenty-two year old marriage on the rocks, and of Sylvia, the dog who turns it all around. *"A delicious and dizzy new comedy."* - *New York Times.* *"FETCHING! I hope it runs longer than Cats!"* - *New York Daily News.* [2M, 2W]

DRAMATISTS PLAY SERVICE, INC.
440 Park Avenue South, New York, New York 10016 212-683-8960 Fax 212-213-1539

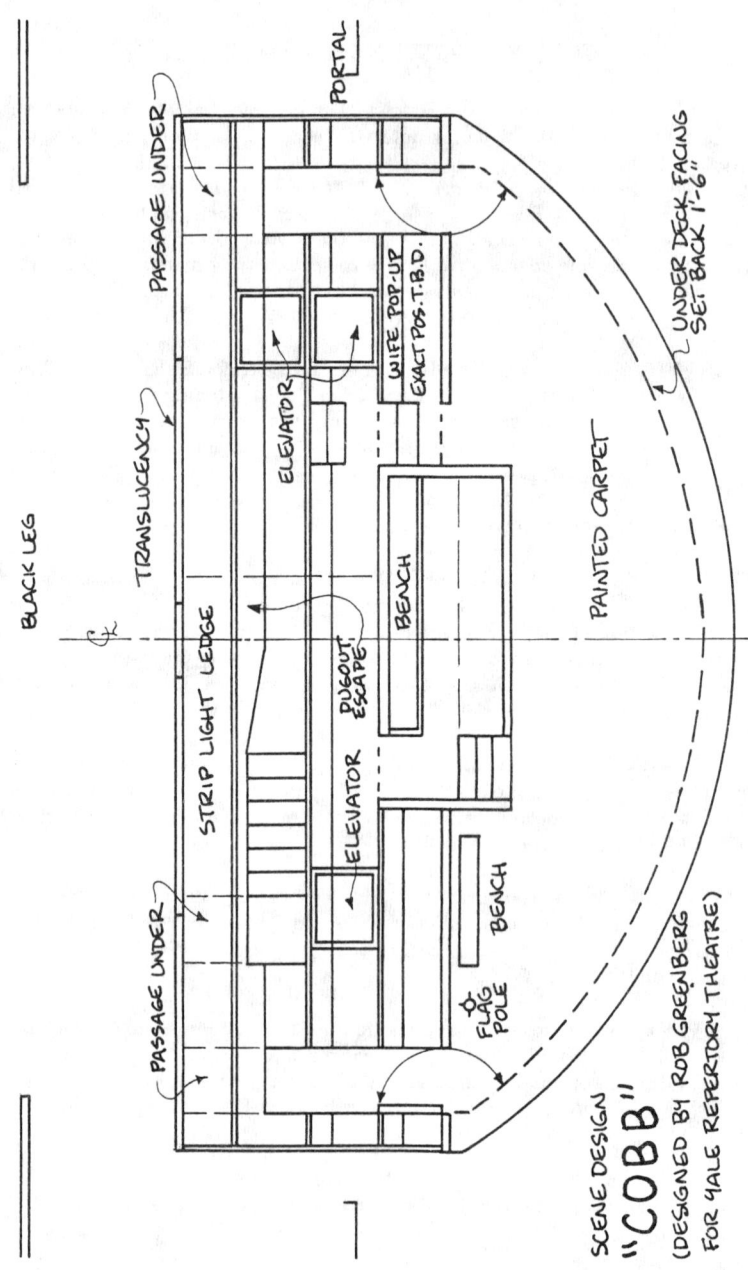